Stress and Depression

Jane Bingham

WAYLAND

First published in 2008
by Wayland

This paperback edition pushlished in 2010 by
Wayland, a division of Hachette Children's
Books, an Hachette UK Company.
338 Euston Road
London NW1 3BH
www.hachette.co.uk

Wayland Australia
Level 17/207 Kent Street
Sydney, NSW 2000

Series editor: Nicola Edwards
Consultant: Peter Evans
Designer: Alix Wood
Picture researcher: Kathy Lockley

The author and publisher would like to thank the following for allowing their pictures
to be reproduced in this publication:
Liam Bailey/Photofusion: 5; Paul Baldesare/Photofusion: 11, 26;Heide
Benser/zefa/Corbis: 7;Bubbles Photolibrary/Alamy Images: 10, 24; Jacky
Chapman/Photofusion: 42; Mary-Kate Denny/Alamy Images: 40; Kevin Dodge/Corbis:
29; Raymond Gehman/Corbis: 23; Gina Glover/Photofusion: 14; Crispin
Hughes/Photofusion: 12; Jupiterimages/Brand X/Alamy Images: 6, Cover
Image100/Corbis: 25; Image Source/Corbis: 16, 20, 37; Leblond/Stockphoto/Alamy
Images: 45; Roy McMahon/Corbis: 30; Mika/zefa/Corbis: 32; Mira/Alamy Images: 33;
Roy Morsch/Corbis: 31; Gabe Palmer/Corbis: 28; Helene Rogers/Alamy Images: 22;
Shoot/zefa/Corbis: 43; Ariel Skelley/Corbis: 9; Christa Stadtler/Photofusion: Titlepage,
36; Tom Stewart/Corbis: 33; Wayland Archive: 4; Wishlist: 8, 17, 18, 19, 21, 34, 38, 41

British Library Cataloguing in Publication Data
 Bingham, Jane
   Stress and depression. - (Emotional health issues)
   1. Stress in adolescence - Juvenile literature
   2. Depression in adolescence - Juvenile literature
   I. Title
   155.9'042'0835

ISBN: 978 0 7502 6169 2

Printed in China

The case studies in this book are based on real experiences but the names we have used are fictitious and do not relate to real people. Except where a caption of a photograph specifically names a person appearing in that photograph, or an event in which real people have participated, all the people we have featured in the book are models.

Contents

Words that appear in **bold** can be found in the
glossary on page 46.

Introduction

Over the past year, Sam has had to cope with a lot of **stress**, and now it's really getting him down. He feels exhausted all the time, no matter how long he sleeps. He just wants to stay in bed and never get up again. He can't face doing anything – not even going out with his friends, and when he thinks of the future he just sees emptiness. Sam has felt sad before, but never like this. He feels completely cut off from his family and friends, and they don't know what they can do to help him.

Sam is experiencing **depression**. All the stresses in his life have combined to make him ill. Depression is an overwhelming sense of sadness and despair. It takes over people's lives and stops them being able to cope with the demands of everyday living. Teenagers who have depression can't just shake it off. They need support to help them recover.

Many cases of depression are triggered by stress, and may be caused by distressing events, such as a **bereavement** or loss or major life changes. As young people enter their teenage years, they encounter a lot of new stresses, and sometimes all these pressures can be very hard to cope with.

Being depressed can make you feel very isolated. But you shouldn't have to cope with your feelings alone.

Depression is not uncommon in the teenage years. Teens from all backgrounds can experience stress and depression.

Find out more

This book gives you the facts about depression. It describes the impact that the illness can have on people's lives and examines the various causes of stress that can lead to depression. Finally, it shows how people can recover from depression, and suggests ways to cope with stress.

Too much stress

No one can avoid stress and pressure. In fact, some pressure can have a positive effect. Many people enjoy the challenge of being under pressure in a match or a competition. But when the stresses build up, it doesn't feel good at all, and it is natural to become anxious. When teenagers experience a combination of stress and **anxiety** they may be vulnerable to becoming depressed.

It's a fact: depression

- Around one in eight teenagers will experience at least one episode of depression before reaching adulthood.
- Episodes of teenage depression generally last about eight months.
- Approximately five per cent of teenagers experience serious, long-term depression.

Chapter 1: What is depression?

People often say they are 'depressed' when they are feeling sad or low. But true depression is different from simply having a bad day or feeling down. Major depression is a serious **mental illness**.

Not just a passing mood

All people have times when they feel low – especially when sad things happen – but usually those feelings don't take over their lives. After a few days or weeks of feeling down, most people manage to get on with everyday activities again. Although they may occasionally feel sad, they know that they can look forward to a future when they will feel better again.

When people experience depression, their feelings of sadness just don't go away. Depression can last for weeks or months, and, in very severe cases, even for years. People who are depressed can't escape from their negative thoughts and they can't imagine a time when they will feel better.

When you are depressed, it can be hard to concentrate on schoolwork. This can lead to extra difficulties, if you fall behind with your studies.

Sadness and despair

Teenagers with depression describe their powerful feelings of sadness and despair. Some of them talk about looking into an endless black hole, and some experience the frightening sensation of being stuck, with no way out. Some very depressed people decide that they can't go on living and attempt **suicide** (see pages 12-13).

Tired all the time

A common symptom of depression is fatigue, or an overwhelming sense of tiredness. Many people who are depressed sleep for hours on end, hardly emerging from their bedrooms at all. They lack energy and may spend many hours sitting in a chair, simply staring into space.

The feeling of exhaustion that often accompanies depression can lead people to drop out of social activities. Some teenagers with depression skip school frequently and may find it very hard to keep up with their schoolwork.

In focus: altered sleep patterns

Depression often affects people's sleep patterns. Some people with depression sleep for very long stretches; others sleep much less than they did before. It is very common for people suffering from depression to wake up early and then be unable to go back to sleep. Depressed people sometimes experience **insomnia**, when they struggle to get to sleep or they wake during the night.

Teens with depression often struggle to get up in the morning. Then they battle with feelings of tiredness throughout the day.

Many teens with depression feel angry and misunderstood. Instead of being able to turn to their family for help, they feel cut off and isolated.

In focus: *aches and pains*

People who are depressed frequently experience headaches or stomach aches. Many say their arms and legs feel heavy and achy.

In some cases, the family and friends of depressed teens become impatient with all their complaints because there is no obvious medical cause for the aches and pains. But the painful sensations that a depressed person feels are very real, and they are often clear symptoms of mental distress.

Anxious and distracted

Many people with depression experience powerful feelings of anxiety. They may become very agitated for no apparent reason, pacing restlessly around the room. They may also feel distracted a lot of the time, and have trouble concentrating. It is very common for someone who is depressed to become much more forgetful than before, and to have great difficulty making simple, everyday decisions.

Feeling angry

In some people, feelings of depression reveal themselves in irritability, anger and hostility. They describe a sense of pent-up rage and frustration. Their angry feelings can make them lash out at their friends and family. Depression can also make teens especially sensitive to criticism or rejection. Teenagers who are depressed may feel as if they are worthless.

Alone and apart

Many teenagers with depression describe their intense feelings of isolation. Just when they are most in need of help, they withdraw from others and become harder to reach than before. If they are told to 'snap out of it' by people who do not understand what they are experiencing, this can deepen their sense of isolation. Many young people who are depressed lose interest in social activities and put up barriers by becoming moody and irritable. As a result, many teens feel that they are forced to struggle with their problems alone.

As their depression becomes more severe, teenagers may retreat further from family life and from their social life with friends. They may spend long periods of time alone and may even run away from home.

Taking risks

Sometimes, being depressed can drive people to take serious risks. Depressed teenagers may start abusing drugs or drinking large amounts of alcohol. They may shoplift, drive recklessly, or engage in unsafe sexual practices. Their risky behaviour is a sign that they are feeling desperate. Without any hope for the future, they simply don't care what happens to them. High-risk behaviour can also be a cry for help.

Teenagers and their parents or caregivers can find themselves in conflict with one another. Relationships within a family are strengthened if people can communicate openly to discuss any disagreements.

Feeling worthless

People who are depressed usually have very low **self-esteem**. They feel that they are worthless and that their lives don't matter. When teenagers become depressed, they may neglect their appearance. Sometimes they stop taking showers and changing their clothes regularly.

Some teens express feelings of despair by engaging in cutting or other forms of self-harm. Any form of self-harm should be taken very seriously.

Some people with depression have strong feelings of self-loathing and guilt. They may believe that they are a burden to their families and others. Sometimes they attempt to deal with their overwhelming negative feelings by engaging in cutting or other forms of **self-harm**.

Self-harm

Many people who self-harm cut themselves with razor blades or burn their skin with lighters or cigarettes. Self-harm is a physical expression of inner pain and an attempt to relieve emotional pressure. It should also be seen as a cry for help. When teenagers harm themselves, they are sending out a clear message of pain and despair.

Changed eating patterns

People who are depressed typically experience changes in their eating patterns. They may express too much or too little interest in eating and have a large weight gain or loss.

Some depressed teenagers restrict their food intake severely in an attempt to change themselves and take control of their lives. Others may turn to food for comfort and eat even when they are not hungry.

Some people who are depressed **binge**, or eat unusually large amounts of food quickly, and then feel terrible

All families have rows, but serious family conflict can often be a trigger for depression.

afterwards. Following binges, they may **purge** their bodies of food by deliberately vomiting or by using **laxatives**.

Abnormal eating patterns can be signs of serious eating disorders, including **anorexia**, **bulimia**, and **compulsive eating disorder**. Eating disorders frequently occur with other mental disorders such as anxiety and depression. It remains unclear whether eating disorders trigger depression or whether people who are depressed are more prone to eating disorders.

CASE STUDY

Max had been having a hard time at home, arguing with his step-dad all the time. Sometimes Max felt so helpless and angry, he punched his bedroom door until his fists bled. At school he started getting into fights and became involved with a crowd of kids who shoplifted for thrills. Max liked the excitement of taking risks because it distracted him from his feelings of sadness and anger. But afterwards he felt worse than before. Fortunately, Max's teacher realized that there was something more behind Max's changes in behaviour. She recognized that he might be depressed.

Thoughts of death

When people have severe depression, they may start to think a lot about death. Depressed teenagers sometimes read poetry about death or listen to music with morbid themes. They may also start to give away their possessions. These kinds of behaviour signal that a person is thinking seriously about death, and the warning signs should not be ignored. When someone is experiencing

Some teenagers with depression withdraw into their rooms, and may even stay in bed all day.

major depression, suicide can be a real possibility.

Suicide and suicide attempts

Depression can cause feelings of despair so overwhelming that suicide seems the only way out. Teenagers who are depressed sometimes feel that death is their only option. In these cases, people usually take great care to make sure that their suicide attempts are successful.

However, there are some people who talk about suicide but who don't truly wish to die. They may threaten to kill themselves or even attempt to commit suicide, but they also make arrangements to be discovered before it is too late. These people are reaching out for help by revealing their desperate feelings. Anyone who threatens or attempts to commit suicide is in urgent need of expert medical help. All suicide attempts should be taken seriously.

Suicide helplines

When teenagers feel suicidal, they need help fast. They can call helplines that are available 24 hours a day and are staffed by trained, experienced **counsellors**. Most counsellors talk to teenagers in complete privacy and confidence. They offer support but do not judge or blame, and they can direct troubled teens to organizations and people who can help. See page 47 for a list of helplines.

It's a fact:
suicide

- Approximately 15 per cent of people with depression die by suicide.
- In the United Kingdom, suicide is the second leading cause of death among teenagers (after road accidents).
- The charity Depression Alliance estimates that each year there are around 19,000 suicide attempts by teenagers in the UK.
- A recent survey of 14-year-olds in the UK showed that more than one in 10 had considered taking their own lives.
- Girls are more likely to attempt suicide, but boys are more than twice as likely to die by suicide.

Chemical changes

Some types of depression seem to be mainly triggered by chemical changes in the brain. Both **seasonal affective disorder (SAD)** and **bipolar disorder** are types of depression that are caused by recognizable changes in the chemistry of the brain.

Seasonal affective disorder

Some people living in northern countries suffer from depression during the winter months. As the days get shorter and the hours of sunlight diminish, people with SAD become depressed. Symptoms include sadness, irritability, changes in sleeping and eating, poor concentration, fatigue, aches and pains, and severe anxiety. The symptoms go away in the spring.

Researchers have discovered that a lack of sunlight affects the chemistry of the brain, and in some people the lack of light triggers depression. The most effective treatment for people with SAD is light therapy for one to two hours a day. Special light boxes

Some people respond to a lack of sunlight by becoming seriously depressed. They have the condition known as SAD (seasonal affective disorder).

Some of the signs below can be indications of depression – especially if they last for more than a couple of weeks. If you or your friends are experiencing two or more of these symptoms, it may be time to seek help.

- sleeping too much or too little
- eating too little or too much
- lack of interest in appearance
- irritability and extreme sensitivity to criticism
- lack of enthusiasm and motivation
- withdrawal from activities with family and friends
- forgetfulness and distraction
- sudden outbursts of temper
- sadness or despair
- drug or alcohol abuse or other risky behaviour
- frequent headaches and stomach pain and generally feeling unwell

with high-intensity fluorescent tubes can be installed in homes to help lessen feelings of depression.

Bipolar disorder

A very small proportion of the population has bipolar disorder, also known as manic depression. People with bipolar disorder experience periods of depression alternating with times when they are very happy and excited, or **manic**.

Bipolar disorder usually develops in the late teens or early twenties. Some people with bipolar disorder experience dramatic mood swings throughout their lives, but others have just a few episodes. Between 20 and 40 per cent of young people who have depression later develop bipolar disorder, according to a report by the surgeon general of the United States.

People with bipolar disorder need expert treatment to control their mood swings. They are usually treated with a combination of **psychotherapy** and prescribed mood-stabilizing medication, such as **lithium**.

Chapter 2: *Under pressure*

There are signs that teenage depression is on the increase. For example, over the last five years, UK surveys have shown a sharp increase in the number of children who are admitted to hospital because they have attempted suicide or practised self-harm. So why is depression growing so fast? Some experts say the increase is a result of the stresses of modern teenage life. Teenagers today are under a lot of pressure – at home, at school, and among their peers. All of these stresses can leave young people feeling helpless, anxious and depressed.

Pressures at home

When children enter their teens, life at home becomes more complicated than before. As teenagers struggle to gain independence, they come into conflict with their parents or caregivers. Family conflicts are perfectly normal, but they can be stressful. Some teens become angry and distressed, and others withdraw from family life and spend a lot of time alone.

If the family conflict continues for a long time, a negative atmosphere can

It's very common for teenagers and their parents to disagree, but these rows can become a serious cause of tension.

After their parents' break-up, teens can be faced with painful situations. A new baby can make the older children feel left out.

build up. In this situation, some teens feel lonely and despairing. Others struggle to cope with pent-up anger and frustration, which can lead to depression.

Family break-up

By the time children reach their teens, many of them have experienced a family break-up. Teenagers may be especially sensitive to family problems and may feel pressure to intervene in the conflict. They also have to deal with the consequences – such as missing one of their parents or coping with a stepfamily. So it's not surprising that family break-up can contribute to depression in young people, particularly if the divorce takes place in an atmosphere of bitterness and anger.

CASE STUDY

When Amy was young, she had a very happy family life. By the time she was 13, however, life at home had changed. Her parents argued a lot, and both of them were very sad and withdrawn. Amy tried her best to make things better, but nothing worked; in the end, her parents decided to divorce. After the break-up, Amy and her sister lived mostly with their mum. Their dad moved in with his new partner and her young sons. In this new situation, Amy felt worried about her mum, who was lonely and angry. Amy also had to get used to a different way of life with her dad and his new family. Amy felt very stressed about all the changes in her life, and she missed the times when her family was still together. She struggled to cope for as long as she could, but eventually she was overwhelmed by feelings of depression.

Reacting to the split

Before a divorce, most families go through a very painful period of conflict. It can be upsetting to teens who hear their parents attacking each other, and see them feeling sad. Some teens try to get involved, and often get hurt in the process. Others make the decision to withdraw, which can leave them feeling miserable and alone.

Teenagers usually experience a mixture of emotions when their parents split up. Often they feel sadness as well as anger about what they've lost. Their loyalties are almost always divided between their parents.

Many teens mistakenly feel guilt about their parents' break-up. Most of all, the young people feel helpless as they watch the world they know fall apart. These reactions can result in depression as teenagers are overwhelmed by their negative feelings.

A new way of life

After a couple has split up, their children's lives can change significantly – and very quickly. Teenagers may have to adjust to living with just one parent, and they often miss the absent parent badly. Children may also have to divide their time between two homes.

Swapping homes is especially difficult and stressful for teenagers, who want to have a social life of their own. Some teens have to move to new homes and attend different schools.

Listening to your parents arguing can be very distressing. Faced with this situation, many teenagers feel helpless and depressed.

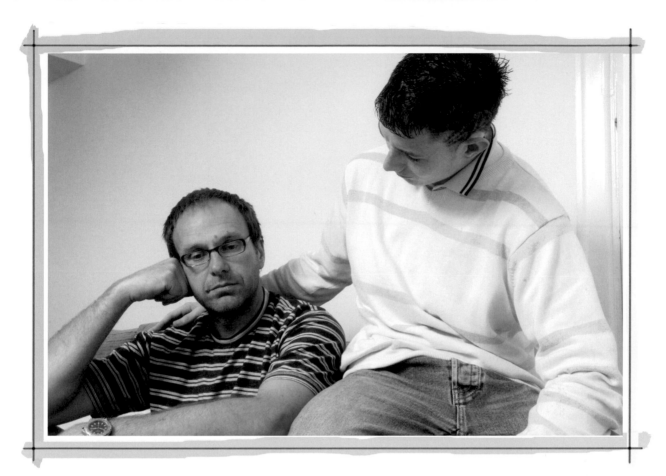

Some teenagers have to cope with their parents' feelings of despair. This can be a difficult burden to bear at a time when they are feeling unhappy too.

Teenagers who live with one parent can struggle with powerful feelings of sadness, anger and blame. They may also feel responsible and anxious for the newly single parent.

If the divorced parent is depressed, sad and angry, the children can experience negative effects and their own feelings of anxiety may be heightened.

In focus: *guilty feelings*

It is common for teenagers to experience feelings of guilt when their parents split up. Children may believe that their behaviour has somehow caused the problem between their parents. These feelings of guilt are natural, but mistaken. Even though there is less of a stigma today about parents separating than there used to be in the past, teenagers can feel sensitive to what other people think. Unless teenagers talk about their emotions, these feelings can lead to depression.

When a parent takes a new partner it can be very difficult for their children. Many teenagers struggle to get used to a new adult in their life.

Changing families

In many cases, the children of divorced parents have to get used to a lot of new people in their lives. Their parents may have new partners, and these partners may have children of their own. Changes in the family's structure can be very stressful.

You're not my parent!

Coping with a parent's new partner can be especially hard for a teenager. Even if the teenager likes the new boyfriend or girlfriend, the child may resent the newcomer for taking the biological parent's place. A young person may find it difficult to have a new adult making the household rules. In addition, a teen may feel uncomfortable about a parent's new sexual relationship at a time when the teen is discovering his or her own sexuality.

Blended families

Many teenagers today live in blended families. Some teens have stepbrothers and stepsisters; some have half-brothers and half-sisters; and others have both. It's also common for children to belong to two blended families, as both of their parents have remarried. While blended families can offer great opportunities for fun, they can also be a source of conflict and unhappiness.

Teenagers sometimes experience strong feelings of resentment towards their stepbrothers and stepsisters. They may feel squeezed out of their old position in the family. They may resent having to share their parent with new children, and they may object to any intrusion into their private space. Faced with new family members whom they dislike, some teens may become hostile. Others cut themselves off from the rest of the family, becoming isolated and lonely.

The arrival of a new half-sibling can help bring a family together. But it can also make the older children feel left out. Some teens say they feel less loved than before because their parents seem to give all their attention to the new child. In this situation, teenagers can sometimes become depressed without their parents being aware of the problem.

Having to share your space with a new step-sibling can leave you feeling angry and depressed – especially when nobody seems to understand your feelings.

It's a fact: divorce and remarriage

- More than one in three marriages end in divorce, and around half of divorces involve children.

- Psychological studies have shown that normal teenage development is threatened by divorce.

- Some children of divorced parents, who had appeared to adjust well early on, experience a re-emergence of problems in their teens. In general boys adjust less well than girls.

Pressures at school

For many teenagers, school can be a very stressful place. Students feel pressure to earn good grades, perform well in sports and other extracurricular activities, and get along with their peers. Some teenagers seem able to take challenges in their stride, but others feel weighed down by the need to succeed.

Being the best

Some schools set high standards, and competition among students may be fierce, both to gain a place at the school and to do well once they are there. Their parents may expect great accomplishments from them, and children may be terrified of letting their families down.

Many pupils also have very high expectations of themselves and blame themselves bitterly if they fail. These students often study for long hours and become excessively worried and anxious about their performance in exams.

Some teens have to juggle after-school jobs with a heavy homework load. They can be overwhelmed with exhaustion and become depressed. Others may attend boarding school and have to cope with feelings of homesickness and loneliness.

Many pupils feel under pressure to do well at school and in exams. Sometimes the stress just becomes too much for them.

Teenagers who aim for success in sport often feel under pressure. If they fail to reach their goals, they can become severely depressed.

Teenagers can feel driven to succeed in many areas besides schoolwork – sports, music and dance, for example. Some young athletes experience great pressure, from their coaches, their schoolmates, their parents and themselves, to perform at their best on the day of a big game or competition.

Exam stress

While most people don't enjoy taking exams, some young people find the experience unbearably stressful. These anxious teenagers may have trouble eating and sleeping in the days and weeks before a big test. They may be physically sick before the exam or feel paralyzed with nervousness, and their anxiety can hamper their performance. Young people who suffer from overwhelming exam anxiety should seek expert help. An extreme reaction to exams can be a sign of deeper, underlying anxieties and problems.

In focus: not smart to look smart?

Some teenagers feel under a lot of pressure not to do well at school, even though they want to. They may think it isn't 'cool' to work hard at school. Students may believe that high academic achievement will make them less popular with their peer group. Teenagers who get good grades at school sometimes encounter teasing, name-calling, and exclusion from groups. Faced with these negative reactions, teens who want to do well sometimes decide to study in secret, resulting in a lot of extra stress.

Peer pressure

By the time they enter their teens, most young people are spending less time with their family and more time with their peers. Teenagers' willingness to **conform** to their parents' expectations lessens as their need for privacy and acceptance by their peers increases. Greater independence can be exciting, but it can be stressful, too. **Peer pressure** is particularly strong during the senior school years.

Many young people experience pressure from their peers to do things they don't really want to do. They may be pushed to try out new experiences, such as smoking, taking drugs, drinking alcohol or engaging in sexual activities. Some students yield to peer pressure because they want to fit in. They fear that refusal will cause them to lose friends and be unpopular. Others, however, decide to take a stand and say no. Sometimes their position is respected; occasionally they end up feeling lonely and misunderstood. In

Sometimes friends can put you in a difficult situation, when they ask you to do things that feel wrong for you.

In focus: *losing friends*

Friendships are often wonderful and rewarding, but they can sometimes be a source of stress. An argument with a best friend can cause distress and loneliness. When one friend decides a relationship is over, the other person may feel confused and angry. Sometimes the loss of a friendship happens when a person moves away or attends a different school. That loss can leave a big emotional hole. Negative experiences with friends can leave teens feeling isolated and depressed.

either situation, teenagers are in danger of becoming depressed as they struggle alone with difficult situations and decisions. They need someone, such as a trusted adult, to talk to for advice and support.

Being left out

Some teenagers have to cope with cruel treatment from their peers, as they are deliberately excluded from groups. Teens sometimes pick on peers who are perceived as 'different' because of their skin colour, their weight, or a physical or mental disability. Such cruel treatment can have very serious emotional consequences. Excluded teenagers may experience loneliness, humiliation and despair, as well as pent-up frustration and rage.

It can be very hurtful when other teenagers laugh at you. Nobody should have to suffer treatment like this.

Bullying

Bullying is one of the hardest things a teenager may have to face. It can take many forms, but it is always mean and frightening.

Bullies are usually expert at not being caught, and they use a range of different methods, such as abusive phone calls, threatening text messages, and embarrassing or insulting comments on Internet sites or in emails.

A bully may focus on a specific characteristic of his or her victim – appearance, voice, race, religion or sexuality, for example.

Teenagers who are bullied can feel that there is no way out. They can feel frightened, angry and desperate.

Bullies usually mock their targets and call them insulting names. They may threaten or carry out violence, and steal or damage other people's possessions. Sometimes a bully spreads rumours about another person.

Teenagers who are bullied can feel that there is no way to escape. They can feel overwhelmed by feelings of fear, frustration and despair. In a few cases, victims of bullying decide that the only way out is suicide.

In focus: *violence in schools*

Students are less likely to be victims of a violent crime at school than away from school. However, any instance of crime or violence at school can have lasting effects, including depression. In recent years, several high-profile acts of school violence, particularly in the United States, have been widely reported in the news media. In the United Kingdom, statistics show that the level of violence in schools is rising. This increase in violence is especially marked among girls. A recent survey of British girls aged between 11 and 15 showed that almost a third had been in at least one physical fight in the previous year.

The presence of weapons at school creates an intimidating and threatening atmosphere. In 2005, about 8 per cent of U.S. students reported being threatened or injured with a weapon, such as a gun or knife, on school property. Many teenagers today report a sense of anxiety, as they no longer feel completely safe at school. Schools have responded by installing metal detectors, adding security officers, and adopting zero-tolerance policies for weapons possession. School officials have also introduced counselling and conflict-resolution programmes and emphasized better communications between school and home.

CASE STUDY

When Amit was 12 years old, he started at a new school, but he found it very hard to fit in. All the other boys stuck together and made him feel left out. Some of the kids at school told him he wasn't wanted and made fun of him because of his religion. They also sent him threatening text messages and posted cruel comments on the Internet.

Amit felt trapped and afraid. Some bullies had warned him that they would 'get him' if he ever reported them to his parents or school officials, so Amit kept his misery to himself. He stayed away from school as much as he could and spent a lot of time alone. He thought often about the cruel remarks and actions of his peers. Amit started to believe all the terrible things the bullies had said about him. He was overcome by negative thoughts and decided that there was no hope for the future. When Amit's dad found the boy trying to cut his wrists, the father realized that his son had a very serious problem. Amit was severely depressed and suicidal.

Changing bodies

As girls and boys enter puberty, their bodies start to change and develop. These years can be difficult, as many young people find it hard to deal with the physical changes. Girls often feel self-conscious about their new shape, especially if they develop earlier than their friends do. Boys may feel embarrassed when they start to sprout hair and their voices begin to break. Meanwhile, teenagers who start puberty late can feel extremely awkward that their bodies have not yet developed. These factors can cause young teens to withdraw and become depressed.

About eight in ten teenagers have acne, a skin condition that can cause breakouts of spots. Acne can be particularly upsetting for young people and can make them avoid social events and settings. Teens with severe acne may experience a loss of self-confidence and self-esteem. A Canadian research study found that even a mild case of acne can result in depression and thoughts of suicide.

As teenagers enter puberty, they have to cope with many changes. They have to get used to their changing bodies, and they need to adjust to all the pressures of relating to the opposite sex.

Sexual pressures

As teenagers develop adult bodies, they start to have sexual feelings. At the same time, they start to attract the attention of the opposite sex. For some teenagers, this sexual attention feels very threatening, and they may withdraw into depression.

When teens start to 'go out' with the opposite sex, a new element of competition can enter their friendships. For example, if two girls compete for the attention of the same boy, their friendship may become strained. Teenagers who are not yet dating can feel left out by friends who are 'couples'. Some teens worry that they aren't 'normal' if they don't have a romantic relationship by a certain age.

Some young people form couples very early. This can put other teens under pressure to do the same.

In focus: pressure to be thin

As girls reach puberty, they start to gain weight and develop some natural curves. At the same time, however, they may feel intense pressure to be slim. Wherever they look – in magazines and movies or on TV – they see super-thin models and celebrities and read advice on dieting. Some teenagers respond to all the pressure by becoming very unhappy about the way their bodies look. Their self-esteem drops sharply, and some teens even develop an eating disorder, such as anorexia or bulimia (see Chapter 1).

Chapter 3: *At risk*

Most experts believe that depression is caused by a combination of physical, psychological and environmental factors. Certain characteristics or events can put some people at greater risk. However, it is important to note that belonging to a high-risk group doesn't necessarily mean that a person will develop depression.

Families under pressure

Some teenagers have to cope with extreme pressures at home. If their parents have a problem with alcohol or other drugs, children may live with high levels of fear and anxiety. Over time, these feelings can develop into a sense of deep depression and helplessness.

In families where a parent has a serious illness, injury or disability, children often have to take on many extra responsibilities. In some cases, the children become their parents' caregivers and spend much of their time at home, missing out on social activities and sometimes even skipping school. Teenagers faced with this sort of pressure can become very lonely and discouraged.

Violence, abuse and neglect

For some children, home is not a safe place. Their parents may treat them or other family members violently. They may experience physical or sexual abuse from another family member or a family friend. Some children are

When children have to take on the role of carer, they can feel overwhelmed by worry and a sense of helplessness.

CASE STUDY

Whenever anyone asked him to play football after school, Rick always said no. He never gave a reason. None of his friends knew that Rick had to rush home to look after his mum. Rick's mother had a disability, and he had been her main caregiver since he was ten years old. She relied on him to shop, cook meals, clean the home and even to lift her into and out of bed. It was a hard job, and Rick often felt worried and burdened by the responsibility. He also felt sad and angry because he thought that his friends wouldn't understand what he was going through. After a while, the other boys stopped asking Rick to do things with them, and he began to stay away from school more and more. Even though he loved his mum, a future spent caring for her seemed very bleak to him. Sometimes he felt so depressed that he could hardly find the strength to look after his mum.

neglected and lack basic necessities such as adequate food and clothing.

All these experiences are deeply distressing and frightening and can cause lasting emotional damage.

Teenagers who are faced with serious problems, such as violence in the home, should never have to cope alone. There are many places where they can turn to for help. (See page 47 for a list of helplines and websites.)

If teenagers try to cope with problems on their own, they can end up feeling severely depressed and even suicidal.

Some teenagers have to cope with violence in the home. In these frightening situations, teens often become withdrawn and depressed.

Stressful events

In addition to all the usual stresses of growing up, some teenagers have to cope with major causes of distress. Certain events, such as the death of a family member, a friend, or a classmate, can cause overwhelming feelings of grief and helplessness. The death of a beloved pet can also leave a teenager feeling very lonely and sad.

Many young people suffer from depression after their parents have split up, and it is common for teenagers to become depressed when they have to move home and leave their old friends behind.

Some teens become depressed following a break-up with a boyfriend or girlfriend. Ending a relationship or being 'dumped' is never easy,

Some teens have to cope with terrible tragedies. In many cases, they need expert support and counselling to help them recover.

especially when the circumstances are widely known among a group of friends.

Many young people are able to cope with the stresses of negative life events and move on. But for others, who may be especially susceptible to depression, the events pile up and the stresses are too great. In these teens, traumatic events may trigger depression.

It can be a great relief to talk about your problems. Sometimes, just talking things over calmly will help you to cope much better with your feelings.

CASE STUDY

After dating for six months, Sonia and Joe broke up. Sonia's family and friends thought she'd soon get over her sadness at the break-up, but three weeks later she was still staying in bed for most of the day. She spent most of the time sleeping or watching TV. She also stopped caring about her appearance and refused invitations to socialize with her friends. Her mum recognized the signs of depression and arranged for Sonia to see a psychotherapist.

Over the next few weeks, Sonia talked with the therapist about the things that were troubling her. Sonia told the therapist that she was still very sad about her parents' divorce, which had occurred four years earlier. Sonia was also worried that she might fail at school. While she was going out with Joe, she had managed to push those concerns to the back of her mind, but now they had overwhelmed her.

With the help of her therapist, Sonia talked about her feelings and worries and grew to understand them better. After a few months, she was feeling better able to cope with her concerns and enjoy life with her friends.

It is common for teens to deal with feelings of sadness by going on a shopping spree. Sadly, this often makes things worse, as they have to cope with money problems too.

Teenagers in trouble

It is not unusual for young people to get into some sort of trouble during their teenage years. Issues can range from difficulties at school to more serious problems such as criminal offences. Some teenagers, particularly boys, may engage in deliberately risky behaviour such as crossing railway lines to spray graffiti or driving recklessly.

Debt stress

Some teens experience money problems and get into debt. A recent survey revealed that almost half of UK teenagers had been in debt by the time they reached the age of 17. The survey also showed that many of these young people had used credit cards to clock up large debts. Research by the UK charity, Samaritans, revealed that teenagers rated problems with money as one of their main worries.

Gambling is on the rise among teenagers, and Internet gambling is an especially serious problem. A growing number of teens get hooked on the excitement of games like Internet poker, but then find themselves in serious debt. Researchers in the U.S. have found that adolescent gamblers are more likely to report depression than teenagers who did not gamble.

Faced with the anxiety of being in debt, teenagers can become very depressed. They need help to cope with their situation and take charge of their own lives again.

Drugs and alcohol

Some young people experiment with alcohol and drugs. Those substances are frequently associated with depression. A recent study by researchers in the U.S. found that 12- to 17-year-olds with depression were about twice as likely to start abusing alcohol or drugs as teenagers who had not experienced depression over the past year. Researchers are not sure whether anxiety and depression lead to alcohol and drug abuse or whether using alcohol and drugs leads to depression.

Teenagers who become **addicted** to alcohol or drugs can experience a tragic downward spiral that may lead to severe depression and even suicide. Young people who reported using alcohol or drugs were more likely to be at risk of suicide than teenagers who kept away from alcohol and drugs.

Teens who abuse drugs or alcohol need professional support to overcome their addiction. Experts estimate that only about 40 per cent of young people at risk of suicide receive mental health treatment or counselling.

The effects of diet

In some cases, diet can be an important factor in causing depression. When teenagers try to

It's a fact: cannabis linked with depression

The use of cannabis is widespread among teenagers, and some people claim that the drug has no serious side effects. Some medical researchers warn, however, that frequent cannabis use may trigger depression, at least among girls. Doctors who surveyed 1,600 teenage girls in Australia, over a period of seven years, published these findings:

- girls who used the drug daily were five times as likely to become depressed and suffer from anxiety as girls who did not use the drug;
- girls who used the drug at least once a week were twice as likely to develop depression as non-users.

survive on a diet that is very high in sugar and fat, they soon become exhausted, headachy and miserable. Certain food **allergies**, such as an **intolerance** of wheat, can also have a powerful effect on mood, making sufferers feel very 'low'.

Girls at risk

Statistics show that girls are twice as likely as boys to develop depression in their teenage years. Experts have offered a number of reasons why girls develop depression more frequently than boys. Some research indicates that girls are more likely than boys to have difficulties accepting the physical changes of puberty. Many teenage girls become extremely self-critical, and low self-esteem can contribute to depression. Changing levels of hormones during the **menstrual cycle** can trigger mood swings.

Studies have shown that teenage girls are more socially oriented than boys. They are more likely to develop close relationships than boys, and they are also more vulnerable to depression if a relationship ends.

In some families, and in society in general, expectations of behaviour are different for boys and girls. Boys are often encouraged to be more assertive than girls. Faced with this double standard, some girls **internalize** their negative feelings, keeping their anger and frustration tightly under control, until these feelings develop into depression.

Studies have shown that teenage girls and boys tend to have different ways of coping with stressful events. It is common for boys to 'act out' or find a way to distract themselves from their problems. Some researchers state that girls tend to dwell on their

Depression is much more common for girls than boys. There may be many reasons for this, but one possible factor is that girls tend to worry more than boys about their schoolwork and exams.

difficulties and can end up feeling helpless and depressed.

A family problem?

Opinion is divided as to whether a tendency to become depressed can be inherited. There is evidence that bipolar disorder tends to run in families. However, it is hard to know exactly what part inheritance plays in depression. If a child with a depressed parent develops depression, is it the result of a family tendency? Or is it a reaction to a difficult situation at home, as the child watches the parent struggling to cope? Most experts agree that although family history can play a part, depression is the result of many factors.

Children who live for many years with a depressed parent are at risk from depression when they are older. However, not all children who have depressed parents go on to develop depression themselves.

In focus: high-risk personalities

Some personality types are especially vulnerable to depression. Young people with low self-esteem can feel a sense of overwhelming despair when they are faced with difficulties. Teenagers who are **introverted** and tend to keep their problems to themselves run a higher risk of becoming depressed than more **extroverted** teens do. Another vulnerable group is that of **high-achievers** or **perfectionists**, who set extremely hard goals for themselves. If they fail to meet their goals, they often blame themselves bitterly and feel distressed and demoralized.

Chapter 4: *Getting help*

Many teenage sufferers from depression make a full recovery, but they need expert help and the support of family and friends. Fortunately, many experienced people who are well qualified to treat depression are available to help.

Taking the first step

The first step on the road to recovery is finding someone to talk to. Some teenagers decide to share their feelings with a parent or caregiver, or another family member or friend. Others prefer to see a school counsellor or a doctor.

Some young people use the Internet or a telephone helpline to find a counsellor who can help them with their problems.

Making the decision to call a helpline can be a very important step towards recovery.

Simply having someone to share thoughts and feelings with can make a person with depression feel much better. For some people with mild depression, talking with a trusted adult can help them emerge from their illness. However, many others need more help before they can recover.

Individual therapy

Most people with depression can be greatly helped by a course of counselling or psychotherapy. Regular sessions may continue for weeks or months, depending on the severity of the depression. During the sessions, patients are encouraged to explore the reasons underlying their depression. They are also helped to cope with their negative feelings.

Expert counselling can help depressed teenagers understand why they feel 'down'. Therapy can also point the way to making positive changes, so that teens no longer feel overwhelmed by their difficulties. Counselling also helps people to recognize and change their own behaviour, which may have contributed to their depression. For example, some depressed teens blame themselves for events that are not their fault.

Counsellors can help people who are depressed develop strategies to cope with stress. They can also teach people how to be more aware of the events, situations and thoughts that trigger their negative feelings, so they can take steps to avoid such situations in the future. Most professional counselling will be conducted in confidence, but if the young person is in danger, the counsellor must tell and involve other agencies, such as the police.

It's a fact:
treatment for depression

- Research has found that only 30 per cent of teenagers suffering from depression receive treatment.
- The consequences of untreated teenage depression can range from severe depression in adult life, problems with crime and substance abuse, to, in some cases, suicide.
- Studies have shown that around half the teenagers who are treated for depression will not become depressed in the future.

Working with others

When a teenager becomes depressed, it can be helpful to bring the family together for some therapy. **Family therapy** enables the family members to explore conflicts and tensions in a safe environment. A therapist can help parents and their teenage children to understand one another's point of view and find better ways to interact.

Sometimes a small group of people with similar problems attend therapy sessions together. **Group therapy** gives patients the opportunity to compare their thoughts and feelings and to support one another in their efforts to get well.

Medication

Sometimes doctors decide that a course of treatment should include medication as well as therapy. A **psychiatrist** or another doctor may prescribe an **anti-depressant** to help lift a patient's mood and maximize the benefits from therapy.

Talking to other people with similar problems can be very helpful in the process of recovery.

Sometimes, a therapist brings parents and children together to discuss their problems. This can be a very helpful way of dealing with conflict in a family.

In focus: *problems with medication*

When patients are severely ill, medication can help to lift them out of the depths of their depression so that they can benefit more from therapy. But doctors try to keep doses of anti-depressants as low as possible and generally prefer not to prescribe medication to younger people. People who take high doses of anti-depressants over a long period can become dependent on the drugs, and find that they are unable to manage without them.

It is also important that anti-depressants are withdrawn extremely slowly. As the patient approaches the end of treatment, the daily dose of drugs must be decreased in gradual steps. Sometimes, when anti-depressants are withdrawn rapidly, the patient can experience powerful feelings of despair. There have been tragic cases of teenagers dying by suicide because they have 'come off' their anti-depressant drugs too fast.

Having a friend to support you can make a big difference to your recovery. Real friends are prepared to listen when you want to talk, and don't just tell you to 'snap out of it'.

Once someone has started a treatment for depression, it's very important to stick to it, even though it can seem hard at times. Attending regular therapy sessions and carefully following a doctor's instructions can help people make good progress towards recovery.

Keeping a journal

Keeping a daily journal of thoughts and feelings can be a great help in achieving recovery. A daily record helps people recognize and understand what triggers their depression or lifts their mood. It also allows them to express their feelings rather than struggling with buried emotions. A journal can also help therapists work with depressed people.

Support systems

When someone is recovering from depression, they need plenty of help and support. There will still be times when they feel down, and it is very important that they have understanding people to talk to. These people may be friends, parents or professionals, or they may be someone at the end of a helpline. The most important thing is that they are reassuring and never tell the person to 'just pull yourself together'.

For some teens, support groups play a valuable role in helping them recover. These are groups of people who have been through depression themselves and recovered.

Eating well

The things you eat and drink can have a powerful effect on your mood, so it is a good idea to take a careful look at your diet. In particular, research has shown that food that is rich in B vitamins can improve your mood, and make you less likely to develop depression. Orange juice, strawberries, leafy green vegetables and wholemeal bread all provide good sources of vitamin B.

Sleeping well

If you are sleeping well, you will greatly help your recovery, and you will cope much better with stress. Try to go to bed and get up at roughly the same time every day. Your body will then get used to its resting routine.

CASE STUDY

Maya had struggled with depression for months. Most of the time, she stayed in her room, and avoided any contact with her family. Whenever she talked to her mum or dad it always seemed to end in arguments and tears. Eventually, Maya agreed that she needed help, and she started having regular therapy sessions.

After resisting at first, Maya found her therapist was easy to talk to, and she began to feel much better about herself. The therapist also held some family sessions, when Maya and her parents worked together to find more positive ways to relate to one other, and gradually a more relaxed atmosphere developed at home.

In this more positive environment, Maya made very good progress. She worked hard at avoiding negative patterns of behaviour, and also tried to concentrate on the positive things in her life. Even though she felt much better, Maya still continued to see her therapist, who helped her to cope with any new difficulties.

Keeping a journal can help you to keep in touch with how you are feeling. It can also help you to 'let off steam'.

Chapter 5: Coping with stress

All people have to deal with stress in their lives, and there are times when the pressures can feel overwhelming. But stress doesn't have to win. There are ways of coping that can help young people to avoid becoming depressed.

Looking after yourself

When you're feeling anxious and overstressed, it's tempting to hide away from the world. But in fact this will make you feel much worse. If you follow a few simple rules to take care of yourself, you will be in much better shape to deal with stress.

Looking after yourself is really just common sense. You need to make sure you get enough sleep and exercise. Take time to eat breakfast in the morning and eat balanced, nutritious meals throughout the day. It can also greatly help your self-esteem if you wear clean clothes and wash your hair. When you make the effort to get out and do things you enjoy, you will discover that you feel more positive about your life.

Staying aware

It's important to recognize when you're getting stressed, or if you are falling into destructive patterns of behaviour. If you sense that you are getting over-anxious, try to make a deliberate effort to slow down and take 'time out'. Make some time in your day when you can reflect and relax. You might choose to take a warm bath or a shower, practise some yoga, go out for a walk, read a book or listen to soothing music. You could do something that you enjoy with your friends.

Go for help

If you feel that the pressures are getting on top of you, don't keep your worries to yourself. Feeling depressed is nothing to be ashamed of, and you should never feel that you have to deal with it on your own. There are lots of people who will understand what you are going through, and who will help you feel better.

You could start by talking to someone in your family, or to another adult you trust, or you could check out the contacts at the back of this book.

In focus: *beating stress*

Here are some ideas for keeping your life as stress-free as possible:

- Take some 'time out' every day to relax and do something you enjoy.
- Cut down on sugary foods, cola and coffee – they will all make you feel "wired" and stressed.
- Avoid cigarettes – although smoking may seem to relieve stress in the short term, within a very short time the feelings of anxiety will return.
- Laugh. Watch a funny film, tell a joke, or read a comic.
- Get plenty of sleep, fresh air and exercise.

- Remove clutter from your life. Organize your room, and throw away unimportant papers on your desk.
- Make a list of all the demands on your time and energy for one week. Give priority to the most important tasks and do those first.
- Break up big projects into smaller, more manageable tasks so you don't feel overwhelmed.
- Create realistic expectations and deadlines for yourself.
- Putting things off adds to feelings of stress. Don't delay doing homework or studying for exams.

- Don't keep your worries to yourself – talk them over with a friend.
- Write down your feelings in a journal – this will make you more aware of the sort of things that make you feel stressed.

One of the best ways to fight off depression is to take plenty of exercise – especially if it involves having fun with your friends!

Glossary

addicted Unable to give something up.

allergy A physical reaction that makes people feel ill.

anorexia An eating disorder, in which people feel an overwhelming need to be thin. Anorexia is short for anorexia nervosa.

anti-depressant A drug that can help to lighten the mood of someone who is depressed.

anxiety Extreme worry.

bereavement An experience of loss, following the death of somebody close.

binge To eat a very large amount of food in a very short time.

bipolar disorder A condition in which periods of depression alternate with periods of feeling 'high'.

bulimia An eating disorder, in which people binge on large amounts of food, and then try to empty their bodies of the food, by vomiting or taking laxatives. Bulimia is short for bulimia nervosa.

compulsive eating disorder An eating disorder, in which people feel an overwhelming need to keep on eating even when they are full.

conform To stick to, or accept something, usually without questioning it.

counsellor Someone who provides support and advice, as part of their job.

depression A powerful sense of sadness, despair and hopelessness. Depression is a serious mental health problem.

extroverted Outgoing and apparently confident.

family therapy Counselling and advice that involves the person experiencing the problem and one or more members of that person's family.

group therapy Counselling and advice that involves two or more people with the same problem.

high-achievers People who usually achieve outstanding results, and who push themselves to do extremely well.

insomnia Difficulty in sleeping.

internalize To keep something hidden and under control.

intolerance Lack of understanding and acceptance.

introverted Shy and not outgoing.

laxatives Substances that cause people to go to the toilet.

lithium A drug that controls mood, preventing people experiencing extreme highs and lows.

manic Very lively and excitable.

menstrual cycle A monthly cycle in which the lining of the womb is shed, resulting in bleeding, or 'periods'. Girls begin the menstrual cycle once they reach puberty.

mental illness A disorder that affects thinking and behaviour.

peer pressure Pressure from people of the same age and in the same situation.

perfectionist Someone who aims to be as perfect as possible in everything that she or he does.

psychiatrist A medically qualified doctor who treats people with mental illness.

psychotherapy The process of helping someone with emotional and/or mental health problems, mainly through talking with them.

purge To get rid of food from the body, by vomiting or taking laxatives.

seasonal affective disorder A mental health problem in which people respond to a lack of sunlight by becoming depressed.

self-esteem Positive feelings about yourself.

self-harm Actions, such as cutting, by which people deliberately hurt themselves.

stress Pressures that make people anxious.

suicide The act of someone killing himself or herself.

Further information

Books to read

Sarah Lennard-Brown, *Stress and Depression* (Hodder Wayland, 2004)

Claire Wallerstein, *Need to Know: Depression* (Heinemann Library, 2004)

Michael Piquemal, Oliver Tossan, Melissa Daly, *When Life Stinks: How to Deal with Your Bad Moods and Depression* (Harry N. Abrams, Inc, 2004)

Ned Vizzini, *It's Kind of a Funny Story* (Miramax Books, 2007)

Bev Cobain, *When Nothing Matters Anymore: Survival Guide of Depressed Teens* (Free Spirit Publishing Inc, 2007)

Telephone helplines

ChildLine
A UK charity dedicated to helping children and teenagers in distress.

Website: www.childline.org.uk/
24-hour helpline: 0800 11 11

Samaritans
A UK charity that provides confidential emotional support to anyone in emotional distress or at risk of suicide.

Website: www.samaritans.org.uk
24-hour helpline: 08457 90 90 90
Email: jo@samaritans.org

Helpful websites

www.youngminds.org.uk
The website of YoungMinds, a UK charity dedicated to improving the mental health of all children and young people.

www.healthyplace.com
This website offers comprehensive information on depression and advice on how family and friends can help a depressed person.

www.nimh.nih.gov/index.shtml
The website of the U.S. National Institute of Mental Health, the world's largest scientific organization aimed at researching into the promotion of mental health and the treatment and prevention of mental disorders. The website offers advice on what to do when a friend is depressed.

www.extension.umn.edu/distribution/youthdevelopment/DA3083.html
The 'Teens in Distress' series of articles on the University of Minnesota's Extension website includes information on adolescent stress and depression and on helping friends in trouble.

www.pamf.org/teen/parents/emotions/depression.html
The website of the Palo Alto Medical Foundation offers information on a range of teen health issues including depression and there are tips for parents on recognising and treating teenage depression.

Index

Page numbers in **bold** indicate pictures.